MW01171893

SAVE THAT PENNY FOR A SUNNY DAY

BY X'ERNONA WOODS

XWOODS ENTERPRISE PUBLISHERS

Published by XWOODS ENTERPRISE
Chicago, Illinois 60649* xernona@gmail.com

International Standard Book Number:
978-0-9823886-0-0

Printed in the United States of America
This is a lead free publication.

- Dedication -

would like to dedicate the success of my book to Christ University Temple for teaching the "DREAM ERIES" that inspired me to create infinite possibilities.

- With Appreciation -

o my beautiful son, Nacalan, who has supported me with lots of hugs and kisses and plenty of iggles that place a smile within my heart. You are mommy's shining example of perfection.

o my mellow nephew, Chii, who is full of wisdom. It is your belief in your Aunt that gives me the trength to live by an example so you can continue to step into your greatness.

o my dear departed mother, Thelma Woods, a woman whose strength, courage and insurmount-ble love inspire me to live life in excellence. Thanks for sacrificing all of yourself to support the roman you created.

o my successful, dare I say, handsome and talented comedian brother, Sherrod. You encourage me o write, and it is through your love and vision that I continue to write.

o my gorgeous twin, Beatrice, who just happens to be four years older, the woman who is forever lacing me on deadline to complete any and every endeavor I dare mention. You are truly the wind eneath my wings. As I write this appreciation, I am remembering the song you dedicated to me by Ielba Moore, "Just Let Me Walk." (No, I did not cry as I wrote my appreciation.)

o my wonderful Aunt Rena Mae, the word "thanks" would never be enough for all the long, late-ight conversations about life. Thanks a million times over for being my rock, especially during the ansition of my mother.

- Purpose of Book -

Save That Penny For A Sunny Day" is an academic component that focuses on Illinois and ational learning benchmarks for reading, mathematics, social studies, and economics. This ook series is designed to increase the ability to understand fundamentals and concepts in hese subject areas. Each page offers students the gateway to explore and challenge their ognitive and critical thinking skills, that will allow substantial growth for generations to ome.

FOREWORD

DOES MONEY GROW ON TREES?

There will always be a demand for money no matter what corner of the world you live in. It seems as if the cliche " Money Makes The World Go Around" proves to be true as evidence of the unfortunate downfall of the economy.

"Save That Penny For A Sunny Day" embraces the areas of economics, finance and budgeting and dispells the thought that the acronym 'ATM' is often defined by a large percentage of youth as 'Automatically Tell Mom.'

"Save That Penny For A Sunny Day" is not the cure but will offer a healing to those who understand what we are taught as youth often shadows our adulthood lives. Being strong stewards of our money is one way to start the healing process one household, one school, one after-school program at a time.

"Save That Penny For A Sunny Day" combined with academic components and national and state standards that focus on reading, math, and social studies to further enrich student learning opportunities while providing inter-related activities to support their cognitive and critical thinking skills.

Students will develop an understanding of how to utilize the teachings within "Save That Penny For A Sunny Day" for a lifetime to come.

After all, Money Really Doesn't Really Grow On Trees.

Mr. Jesse White
Secretary of State

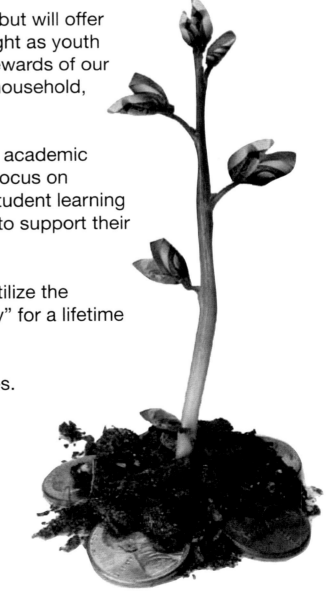

Hello, I am Mrs. Sanders. I am going to tell you a story about turning a dream into reality.

There was a six-year-old boy named Karim who helped his Aunt Delores make special treats.

Every summer he went to his Aunt's house and they made their special lemonade.

It was special because of their secret ingredient.

Everyone loved the delicious lemonade. As fast as Karim and Aunt Delores stirred, it was gone!

ICEcol Lemona

5108 Main Street
Karim's Lemonade

All of his family and neighbors loved to drink Karim's lemonade on warm, sunny days.

One hot summer day, Karim thought it would be a great idea to start a **business**.

"But what kind of business?" Karim asked himself.

Karim pondered for a while. Then all of a sudden he looked up at the sky and shouted, " **A LEMONADE STAND BUSINESS!**"

SUNNY DAY FACTS / QUOTES
You are as only good as your word.

6

He ran to his Aunt's house from the park to tell her about his great idea.

When Aunt Delores heard the news, she began to smile. Then she began to stare. Aunt Delores always stared when she thought deeply.

"Where are you going to get the money to start your business, Karim?"

He pointed his finger at her and said,
"From you, of course!"

She saw the joy in his eyes as he pointed.

He knew she would not give him the money, but she would **LEND** him the money.

Karim sat down at the kitchen table when Aunt Delores asked him to write down a list of ingredients.

Karim also compared prices for each item in the lemonade recipe.

Then Aunt Delores asked him to list the customers or **target markets** that would be interested in buying his lemonade. She also wanted him to find a location for his business and add up his operating expenses.

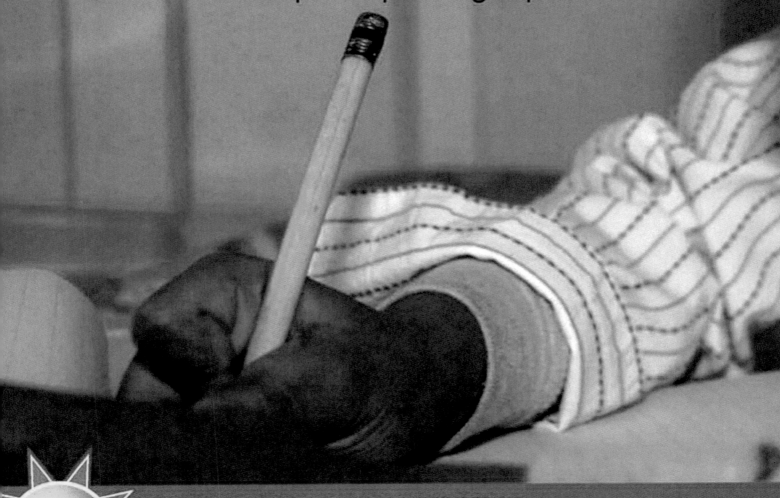

SUNNY DAY FACTS / QUOTES

You get back what you give back.

Karim finished the lists. Aunt Delores reviewed the lists and added the finishing touches for Karim's business plan.

In just one week Karim's **net gain** was a whopping five hundred dollars. Karim was quite happy and wanted more customers to buy his lemonade so that his business would grow.

Aunt Delores thought for a while. Then she called her best friend, Angie, who was a marketing consultant. Karim asked why she had called Angie. Aunt Delores said she had been "networking."

Karim began to put flyers all around town to advertise his awesome lemonade. Soon the word was all over town. People were buzzing about Karim's sweet and sour lemonade.

SUNNY DAY FACTS / QUOTES

If at first you don't succeed, try, try again.

As the summer months passed his **profits** increased. Karim pondered about what to do with his **money**.

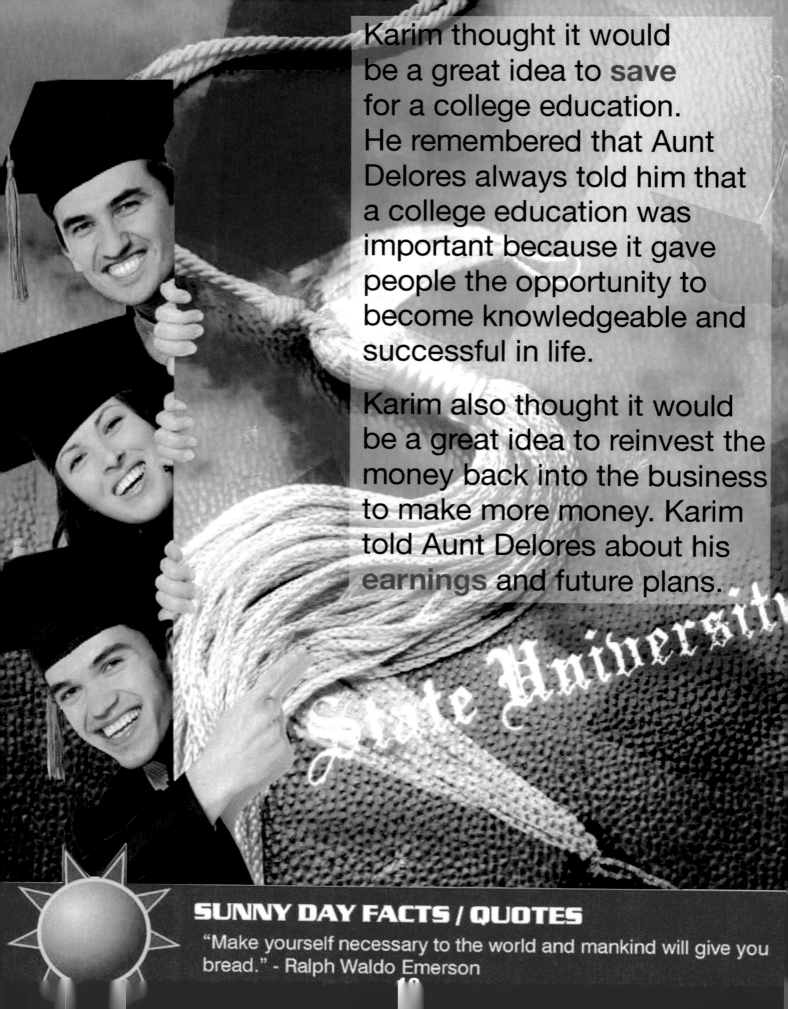

Karim thought it would be a great idea to **save** for a college education. He remembered that Aunt Delores always told him that a college education was important because it gave people the opportunity to become knowledgeable and successful in life.

Karim also thought it would be a great idea to reinvest the money back into the business to make more money. Karim told Aunt Delores about his **earnings** and future plans.

SUNNY DAY FACTS / QUOTES

"Make yourself necessary to the world and mankind will give you bread." - Ralph Waldo Emerson

Aunt Delores called Mr. Ferguson, a **certified financial planner**, and asked him to meet with Karim to teach him how to save and **invest** his money.

Mr. Ferguson advised that he shop around for the best rates and lowest banking fees to receive a large return.

After negotiating their financial **goals**, Karim received an important phone call from an investor who tasted his lemonade.

Karim special sweet and sour lemonade was marketed throughout the United States of America. Karim was filled with excitement.

BANK CARD

0000 0000 0000 0000

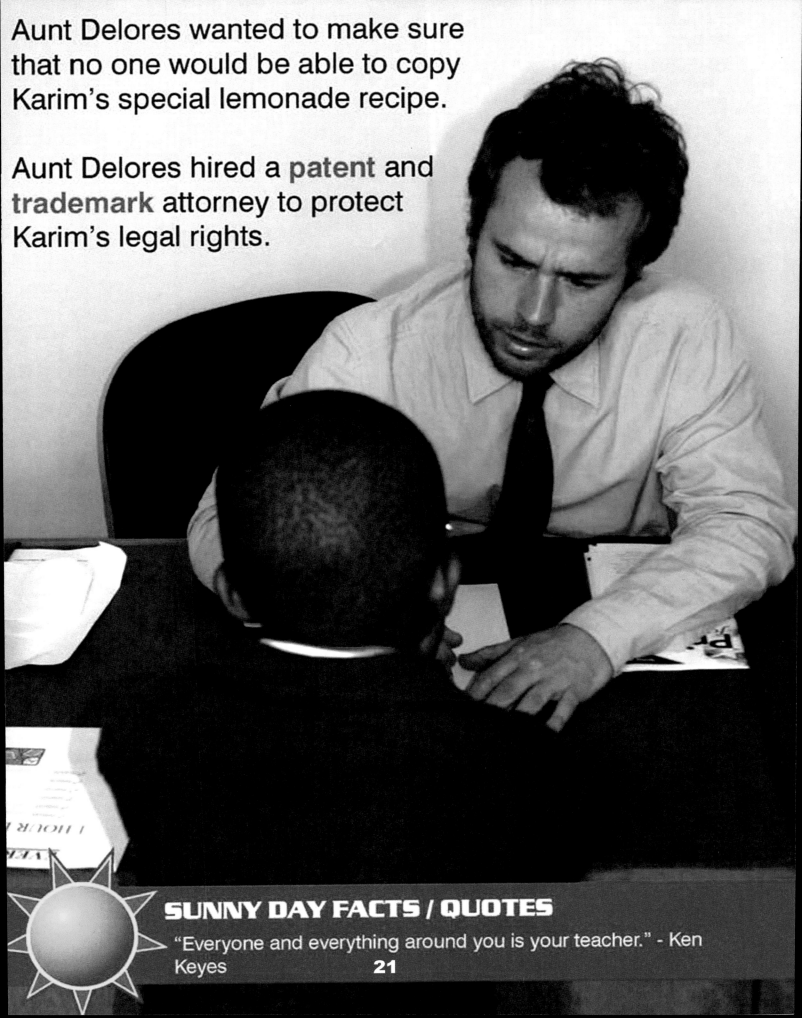

Aunt Delores wanted to make sure that no one would be able to copy Karim's special lemonade recipe.

Aunt Delores hired a **patent** and **trademark** attorney to protect Karim's legal rights.

Karim invested in various **investment portfolios** and built the wealthiest beverage company in the world.

SUNNY DAY FACTS / QUOTES

Perserverance makes the difference between success and defeat.

23

If you have an idea and you truly desire
to start your own business

Invest in your future by studying.
Utilizing your creative ideas.
Collect your resources.
Become knowledgable of your business.

Remember one person's dream could be your reality.

Believe in yourself!

If you can dream it, you can achieve it!

Save That Penny For A Sunny Day
- Glossary Terms -

Advertise - To give public notice of, to announce publicly, especially by a printed notice; such as, to advertise goods for sale.

Business - Any particular occupation or employment engaged in for livelihood or gain.

Business plan - A document prepared by a company's management, detailing the past, present, and future plans of the company, usually designed to attract capital investment.

Certified Financial Planner - A professional who forges a detailed plan: a set of action steps that outline how a client's finances can best be managed.

Earnings - Salary or wages. Business profits. Gains from investments.

Expenses - Overhead charges (accounting), costs of doing business.

Goals - The purposes toward which an endeavor is directed: objectives.

Ideas - Thoughts or concepts, that potentially or actually exist in the mind as a product of mental activity. An opinion, conviction, or principle; a plan, scheme, or method.

Invest - To commit money or capital) in order to gain a financial return: invested their savings in stocks and bonds.

Investment Portfolio - The group of investments held by an investor, investment company, or financial institution.

Lend - To give or allow the temporary use of something on the condition that the same or its equivalent will be returned. To provide money temporarily on condition that the amount borrowed will be returned, usually with an interest fee paid in addition to the amount of the loan.

Marketing consultant - Professional who specializes in the commercial functions involved in transferring goods from producer to consumer.

Money - A medium that can be exchanged for goods and services and is used as a measure of value on the market. Included among its forms are commodities such as gold, an officially issued coin or note, or deposit in a checking account or other readily liqueafiable account.

Net gain - Remaining money after all deductions have been made for expenses; also called net profit.

Networking -To interact or engage in informal communications with others for mutual assistance or support and exchange of information, tips, and suggestions.

Patent - A grant made by the federal government that confers upon the creator of an invention the sole right to make, use, and sell that invention for a set period of time.

Profits - The return received on a business undertaking after all operating expenses have been paid.

Reinvesting - To invest capital or earnings again, especially to invest income from securities or funds into additional shares. Return the profit made on an exchange of goods into the business.

Save - To accumulate money in a fund for a purpose, such as for a college education.

Target market - Identified potential buyers, consisting of a vaguely defined group of people who might buy your products, and their locations.

Trademark - A peculiar distinguishing mark or device affixed by a manufacturer or a merchant to his goods, the exclusive right of use is registered by the federal government and recognized by law.

- WebLinks -

Jumpstartcoalition.org
The jumpstart coalition is an organization dedicated to teaching students money management, saving and investing and proper use of credit.

Moneyopolis.com
Based on National Council of Teachers Mathematics standards. Ernst and Young present this interactive game for middle schoolers that integrates math and social studies into the study of banking. You must register to play (it's free)

Students start with $600 and try to make it grow to $1,000 by the end of the game. Along, the way of getting a job, banking, shopping and paying taxes all come into play.

Lemonadestandgame.com
The lemonade stand game teaches basic math and business skills kids love making a big profit and selling lemonade.

- Entreprenuers who support your Save That Penny For A Sunny Day Dreams. -

Black Pages International
Eugene Dillanado
400 W. 76th, Suite 112, Chicago, Illinois 60620
(773- 783-2700)

Park National Bank
310 N. Pulaski, Chicago, Illinois 60624

Le Collezion
1936 S. Wabash, Chicago, Illinois 60616

Satisfaction Beauty Salon
Di Su Owens
746 E. 43rd, Chicago, Illinois 60653
(773 924-5705)

220 Communications and Kreations Art
Glenn Murray
glenn@kreationsart.com
(866-533-9884)
www.kreationsart.com

Builders Circle
Jovan Jarrett and Charles Sawyer
7419 S. Cottage Grove, Chicago, Illinois 60619
(773-536-0641)

First National Mortgage Sources
Raymond Fleming
6803 South Ashland Avenue, Chicago, Illinois 60636
(773-476-6959 or 773 401-7221)

Chicago Allied Health and Medical Professions
Dr. Jones
3424 S. State Chicago, Illinois 60653
(312-567-3000)

3 Net Wise
Sherrod Woods

Levels of Learning Home Daycare School
Beatrice Cooper
437 E. 46th Place Chicago, Illinois 60653

Artistic Impression
Agnes Davis
Matteson, Illinois

Cafe 917 Liu
917 E. 79th Street, Chicago, Illinois 60619

Freedom Salon
1518 N. Ashland, Chicago, Illinois 60622

Soul Salon Spa
4256 S. Cottage Grove, Chicago, Illinois 60653

ABOUT THE AUTHOR

X'ernona T. Woods the author of "Save That Penny for a Sunny Day" is an author, educator and speaker. This book inspires young readers to think about entrepreneurship, making and saving money, and encourages them to dare to live their dreams. She teaches the "Save That Penny for a Rainy Day" workshop at Carter G. Woodson a University of Chicago charter school in their after-school, Excel program

Ms. Woods, a Chicago native, received her degree in Pre-Medical Biology from Dillard University in New Orleans, Louisiana. Since graduating, Ms. Woods has committed herself to working with youth in non-traditional settings, teaching biology, anatomy and physiology; creative writing and poetry; and economics.

She has served as a mentor with Chicago's Mayor Richard Daley's, workforce development program. Ms. Woods has participated in several life-coaching workshops and has memberships in the Society of Children's Book Writers and Illustrators, National Association of Black Journalists, Youth Biz Entrepreneurs of Women Business Development Center, and Delta Sigma Theta Sorority, Inc..

Ms. Woods is also a partner with Chicago's Federal Reserve, "Money Smart Week."

Ms. Woods is in pursuit of her medical degree with a specialty in Pediatrics. She is a longtime member of the Illinois Institute Chicago Allied Health and Medical Program.

Ms. Woods is vibrant and committed to the belief that we can ignite youth to move mountains and to embark upon new paths of life to lead happier, more fulfilling lives. Her belief in life stands firms that delays are not denials.

Ms. Woods is due to release her next children's book " Dream Big" based on the life of President Barack Obama in the fall of 2009. She is also the instructor and creator of the "It's All About You" workshop and workbook.

To book Ms. Woods for speaking engagements or to order more books, write her at xernona@gmail.com.